# Cuisine
# From Coorg

To
*beloved Kuttaiah*
*who taught me*
*the niceties and refinement*
*of*
*Coorg cuisine*

**Published by**
**Sterling Publishers Private Limited**

# Cuisine
# From Coorg

RANEE VIJAYA KUTTAIAH

A Sterling Paperback

**STERLING PAPERBACKS**
An imprint of
Sterling Publishers (P) Ltd.
A-59, Okhla Industrial Area, Phase-II,
New Delhi-110020.
Tel: 26387070, 26386209; Fax: 91-11-26383788
E-mail: sterlingpublishers@airtelbroadband.in
ghai@nde.vsnl.net.in
www.sterlingpublishers.com

*Cuisine from Coorg*
© 2000, Sterling Publishers (P) Ltd.
ISBN 81 207 2109 8
Reprint 2006

*Published by* Sterling Publishers Pvt. Ltd., New Delhi-110 020.
*Lasertypeset at* Vikas Compographics, New Delhi-110 020.
*Printed at* Sterling Publishers Pvt. Ltd., New Delhi-110 020.
*Cover design by* Sterling Studio
*Photography by* M. Bhaskar

# CONTENTS

# INTRODUCTION

## THE COORG OR THE KODAVA

The Kodavas (Coorgs — a race in Karnataka, India) have regal features, and are tall, strong and beautiful. They are well known for their hospitality. They are Hindus, but not of an orthodox type. Their men wear the *kupya* (a tunic in black and white) and have a sword, either a *peeche kathi* (knife studded with gems) or an *odikathi* (a big cutting sword). The women wear a saree, but differently. The Kodavas are the only community who are exempt from the Indian Arms Act.

A rare feature in Kodava women and men is that they personally serve the food and no servants are allowed to do this. Women are served first at all ceremonies and the men eat after that.

Coorg food is entirely different in taste, flavour and texture and eating a Coorg meal is an experience by itself. Coorgs are very cautious about handing over their recipies and keep them secret. These recipies have been handed down from generation to generation and they have all been tested in Coorg kitchens. Coorgs are mostly non-vegetarian, although they have some delicious vegetarian dishes too.

They cultivate paddy, coffee, cardamom, oranges, pepper and bamboo and they eat pork (home-bred pigs), sheep, chicken and fish.

Different from any other form of Indian cooking, Coorg food makes the palate tingle and titillates the taste buds. Once tasted, this food can never be forgotten.

# KANNE

# Yarchi Nad Kanne

### INGREDIENTS

*1/2 kg mutton bones with a little meat over them 1/2 kg*

*1 large chopped onion*

*2 big chopped tomatoes*

*1 tbsp peppercorns powdered coarsely*

*1 full garlic chopped*

*1 tbsp oil*

*1/2 tsp turmeric*

*1 tsp coriander powder*

*1/2 tsp cumin powder*

*4 cups water*

*salt to taste*

### METHOD

1. Place pressure cooker on fire. Pour in the oil. When hot put in onion, garlic, tomatoes, salt, mutton bones and water. Pressure cook for 20 minutes. If the water is less, add more and make it into a broth. Serve hot.

# Thick Kodava Kanne

This kanne is meant to be eaten as gravy with plain rice.

## INGREDIENTS

| |
|---|
| 2 tbsp tuvar or arhar Dal |
| 1 tbsp oil |
| 1/2 cup coconut grated |
| 1 tsp tamarind pulp |
| 4 dry red chillies |
| 1/2 tsp turmeric |
| salt to taste |
| 2 tbsp jaggery |
| 1/4 tsp mustard seeds |
| 1 medium-sized onion chopped into small pieces |
| 1 sprig curry leaves, |
| 4 cups water |

## METHOD

1. Boil the tuvar dal in a vessel with 4 cups of water. Lower the heat. When the dal is medium cooked, strain the water.

2. Grind the dal with coconut, tamarind, red chillies, turmeric, jaggery and salt into a chutney-like paste.

3. Mix the paste with the dal water into a smooth consistency.

4. In a vessel, add oil and when hot put in mustard seeds, curry leaves and chopped onion. Fry lightly. Add the dal water and bring to boil.

5. Serve with rice.

# Belai Kanne

4 tbsp tuvar dal

6 cups water

1 full garlic peeled

1 big onion chopped

1/2 tsp pepper powder

1 big tomato chopped

salt to taste

2 tsp oil

a little asafoitida

## METHOD

1. Put in pressure cooker all the ingredients, leaving aside a tsp of garlic and onion for seasoning. Add one tsp oil and cook for 10 minutes.

**Seasoning:**

1. In 1 tsp oil, add the balance onion and garlic, both chopped, Pour in the dal mixture and bring to boil.

2. Serve in cups.

# Mallu Kanne

### INGREDIENTS

1 tbsp oil

2 tsp coriander seeds

3 dry red chillies

1 tsp tamarind

2 pods garlic

1/4 tsp cumin seeds

4 cups water

salt to taste

1/8 tsp turmeric powder

small piece jaggery

2 tsp peppercorns

for seasoning:

1 sprig curry leaves

2 cloves garlic crushed

1/2 tsp mustard seeds

1/4 tsp methi (fenugreek) seeds

### METHOD

1. In a vessel pour 1 tsp oil and fry all the ingredients.
2. Grind the mixture into a smooth paste. In cold water, mix the ground ingredients.

**To season:**

1. In a vessel add the balance oil and put in the seasoning. When brown, add the mixed water, put in salt and bring to boil.

*This can be drunk as a soup or eaten with plain white rice. This soup is very good for a bad cold, cough and fever.*

# Nalla Mallu Kanne

### INGREDIENTS

*1/2 kilo mutton bones or*

*1/2 kilo chicken bones*

*1 tsp pepper coarsely ground*

*1 full garlic peeled.*

*1 big onion chopped.*

*6 cups water*

*salt to taste*

### METHOD

1. In a pressure cooker add all the ingredients and cook for 25 minutes.
2. Strain the liquid and serve in cups.

*This is a very good brew for the sick or after confinement and also as everyday soup.*

# PUTTUS

# Puttus

**Rice Preparation:**

6 cups  thari (broken rice)

4 cups podi (rice flour)

### METHOD

1. Wash 10 cups of raw rice in cold water, strain well and dry the washed rice in the sun. (It takes two days to dry well).

2. In a mixer-grinder grind 6 cups of rice for 1/2 a minute or less. The broken rice should be a little bigger than mustard seeds, Sieve and keep the *thari* separately.

3. The balance of four cups rice should be well powdered to make into rice flour. Add the sieved flour to this flour.

*Keep both separately in air-tight containers. It will last for a month or two.*

# Thaliyaputtu

### INGREDIENTS

*1 cup raw rice*

*3 tbsp urad dal*

*1/4 tsp methi seeds*

*1/2 cup cooked rice*

*salt to taste*

*2 tsp sugar*

*1/2 tsp soda*

### METHOD

1. Soak the first 3 ingredients in cold water for 4 to 6 hours.

2. Drain the water and in a mixer grind all the ingredients except the soda with very little water.

3. Keep it covered overnight to ferment. Next morning mix the soda in a little milk and mix it well with the paste. Leave it for half an hour. Spread it on a stainless steel plate and steam it for 20 minutes. When cool cut into pieces of medium size and eat it with Coorg chutney. It can be eaten with a vegetable stew or mutton and chicken curries.

# Papputu

### INGREDIENTS

1 cup broken rice (thari)

11/2 cup water

1/2 cup milk

1/2 grated cononut

3 cardamoms (powdered)

1 tsp sugar

salt to taste

### METHOD

1.  Mix 1/2 cup of thari with 3/4 cup water and 1/4 cup milk. Add the grated coconut, some cardamom, sugar and salt. Mix the contents and pour the mixture into a greased thali.

2.  Repeat this process and fill another thali. Steam for 20 minutes. Take it out and cool. When cool, cut into triangular pieces.

*Eat with curries. This is a luncheon or dinner speciality.*

# Akki Ooti

*2 cups of cooked rice (old rice can be heated)*

*salt to taste*

*rice flour*

**METHOD**

1. Grind the rice and make it into a smooth paste. Knead the rice flour with the paste, adding salt. Do not add water at all. Make chappatis from the dough. The ootis should puff up. Do not add ghee. Eat with rajma curry or til chutney.

# Kadadambuttu

### INGREDIENTS

1 cup thari

1/2 cup of cold water

salt to taste

2 cardamoms (powdered)

1 tsp oil

### METHOD

1. Mix the thari, water and salt together, simmer on a slow fire and stir it gently, Cook the mixture till the water evaporates.

2. Apply oil on the palms and while the mixture is still hot roll it into medium sized balls.

3. In a steamer, spread a wet cloth and arrange the balls on the cloth, Fold the cloth, put on the lid tightly and steam for 15 minutes.

*Eat it with chutney or Coorg (pandi) pork curry, ghee or honey.*

# Nulluputtu

*1 cup thari*

*2 cups of water*

*salt to taste*

*3 cardamoms (powdered)*

**METHOD**

1.  Heat water in a vessel till medium hot. Put in the thari and mix gently, See that lumps are not formed. Cook the thari till it hardens. Remove from the fire. Dipping your hands in cold water, make apple-sized balls. When cool press each ball into a press (which has been oiled) onto a saucer and transfer them to a platter. Repeat till all the balls are finished, and the string hoppers are all made.

# Coorg Yarchi Pulav

Pulav is a grand dish made when visitors come or there is any celebration like childbirth, marriage or an engagement.

## INGREDIENTS

6 cups rice (long grained)

1 kg mutton (cut into medium-sized cubes)

salt to taste

**Masala to grind:**

2 tsp coriander seeds

2 tsp chilli powder

1/4 tsp turmeric powder

1 tsp pepper powder

1/4 tsp jeera (cumin seeds)

1 inch piece cinnamon

4 cloves

3 cardamom

1 tsp khus khus (poppy seeds)

juice of 1 lemon

**For seasoning:**

1/2 cup ghee

1/2 cup dalda

**To grind separately:**

1 full garlic, peeled

4 green chillies

1 big piece ginger

*1 medium bunch of corriander leaves*

*3 stalks of mint leaves*

*2 large onions chopped*

*1 large onion*

**PREPARATION OF MUTTON**

1.  In a pressure cooker, pour dalda and ghee. Add the chopped onion and fry till medium brown, Then add the green masala and fry well. Add the other masalas. Add mutton and fry well, adding a little water. Add salt and pour in 2 1/2 cups water and pressure cook it for 18 to 20 minutes, depending on the mutton.

2.  Uncover and add the lemon juice. The gravy must be thick and the oil should float on top. Keep the lid closed.

**PREPARATION OF RICE**

1.  Wash and soak the rice for 1 hour.

2.  Boil water and add 2 cardamoms and salt and put in the rice. Cook it till it is 3/4 done. Strain the rice, and put it on a thali or a large plate, Add the mutton masala and gently mix the mixture with a fork. Put it back into the vessel and seal the lid with flour paste.

3.  Heat the oven and leave the rice in it for 1 hour. Open and serve it hot. If you do not have an oven, on medium heat, keep a tawa and keep the degchi on it for 1/2 an hour, or cover with a lid and steam in an idli vessel.

# Naikulu

Soak 2 cups of long-grained rice.

## INGREDIENTS

| |
|---|
| *1/4 cup raw cashewnuts.* |
| *1/4 cup raisins* |
| *1 long cinnamon broken to pieces* |
| *4 cloves* |
| *1 cup of ghee and dalda (mixed)* |
| *6 cardamom* |
| *3 full garlic pods (peeled and slit) lengthwise* |
| *3 large onions sliced finely* |
| *2 tsp sugar* |
| *salt to taste* |
| *4 cups of water* |

## METHOD

1. In a vessel, pour 1 cup of ghee / dalda. When it is hot, put in the cinnamon, cloves and cardamom, When brown, add onion and garlic and fry lightly. The onion and garlic should not turn brown, Add the cashewnuts and raisins and fry. Add rice, salt, sugar and water. Cover and cook till the rice is dry and soft and the ghee floats a little on top.

2. Eat with chicken pepper fry, mutton curry or any other vegetable curry.

**Assorted Puttus**

Pandi Curry

# Kodagu Mooru Kulu

2 cups raw rice

2 cups set curd (not sour)

2 onions (chopped)

1 green chilli (chopped)

salt to taste

1/2 piece ginger (sliced)

## METHOD

1.  Mix the medium cooked medium hot rice with curds, salt, ginger, green chillies and onion.

2.  Cool the rice mixture. It goes well with chicken fry or pickles of any kind.

# Ragi Ambulee

## INGREDIENTS

*1 cup ragi flour*

*1/2 cup rice*

*salt to taste*

*6 cups of water*

## METHOD

1. Mix 3 cups of water and ragi flour. Keep overnight to ferment.
2. Next morning, cook the rice in 3 cups of water.
3. After the rice is cooked, add the ragi flour mixture to the kanji (rice water) and keep stirring. Do not allow it to form into a lump. Add more water if necessary, for the ambulee must be medium thin. Add salt and cook the ragi well.
4. Add sour curds and eat it for breakfast with lime pickle.

*It is very good for health and removes all toxins and excess fluid from the body.*

# PANDI

# Pandi Chootad

### INGREDIENTS

*1 kg pork with skin and fat*

*salt to taste*

*juice of 4 lemons*

*or*

*the juice of 2 marmalada oranges*

*8 green chillies or birds eye chillies or khandari chillies*

### METHOD

1. Mix the pork pieces with salt.
2. On a barbeque or on a hot coal oven, or in oven or grill, pierce the pork pieces with skewers and grill them. Keep turning till the meat is cooked and becomes dark brown in colour.
2. Take off the pork pieces from the skewers and put them on a plate. Add green chilli paste and the citrus juice and mix well.

*Best eaten as hors-d'oeuvres (appetizers).*

# Pandi Chops

1 kg pork double chops with skin and fat

*1 kg pork (chops)*

*1/2 tsp turmeric*

*3 large full garlic*

*1 large onion*

*1 long piece ginger*

*8 green chillies*

*1 bunch (medium) coriander leaves*

*1 1/2 tsp peppercorns*

*1 1/2 tsp cumin seeds*

*3 red chillies*

*salt to taste*

*3 cups water*

*kachiyapulli to taste or vinegar*

*or*

*2 lemons or ground cocum*

1 tbsp oil

## METHOD

1. Pressure cook the chops in turmeric and salt with water for 15 minutes. When the chops are cooked, dry the gravy.

2. In a vessel heat the oil, fry the green masala well till the masala is well fried.

3. Add the pork chops and lemon or vinegar or kachiyapulli to taste, and keep frying till dry.

# Chillkana Pandi

## INGREDIENTS

*1kg pork with fat and skin cut into small pieces*

*1/2 tsp turmeric*

*salt to taste*

*3 cups water*

*2 tsp oil*

*2 whole large sliced garlic*

*2 large onions sliced*

*4 pieces green chillies (halved)*

*1 long piece ginger*

*2 tsp pepper powder*

*kachiyapulli or tamarind pulp to taste*

## METHOD

1. Pressure cook the pork with turmeric , salt and water for 10 minutes and dry the gravy completely.

2. In a frying pan pour oil and when hot fry onions, garlic, ginger, green chillies, pepper powder. Add the pork and the tamarind pulp or kachiyapulli.

3. Keep stirring till dry till the pork becomes reddish in color.

4. Remove from fire and serve.

# Pandi Curry

*1 kg pork with skin and fat*

*(Cut the pork into medium sized pieces. Wash well with vinegar and salt. After washing add salt and turmeric and mix well).*

*Dry masala for storing in an air-tight bottle.*

*(This masala can be used four times. It should be kept dry and fresh.)*

### INGREDIENTS TO POWDER

*1 cupful coriander seeds*

*1 tbsp cummin seeds*

*2 tbsp black pepper*

*1 piece cinnamon*

*4 cloves*

*2 cardamom*

*2 red chillies*

*1 tbsp poppy seeds*

*1 tbsp mustard seeds*

*1/8 tsp fenugreek (methi) seeds*

*2 tsp raw rice*

## METHOD

1. Roast coriander seeds till they turn dark brown, (almost the colour of coffee powder.)
2. Roast the jeera, pepper, red chillies, mustard seeds, rice, methi, cardamom, cloves and cinnamon. When light brown, add the poppy seeds. Remove from fire and cool the masala.
3. Dry grind everything into a coarse powder, cool and store in the bottle.

**To make curry (roughly ground green masala)**

<u>INGREDIENTS</u>

*1 large piece ginger*

*1 large onion*

*10 cloves garlic*

*1 medium bunch coriander leaves*

*6 green chillies.*

*kachiyapuli (Coorg vinegar)*

*or*

*8 cocum ground into paste or tamarind pulp*

*2 cups water*

*salt to taste*

**METHOD FOR THE CURRY**

1. Mix the pork with the roughly ground green masala and 3 tbsp of roasted masala . Mix well and decant the pork into the pressure cooker. Add 2 cups of water , cook for 15 minutes. The gravy should not be very thin.

2. Add kachiyapulli. In case it is not available, add ground cocum or 1/4 cup of tamarind pulp.

3. Add more salt to taste. Dry fry it till a thick gravy comes to the surface and the oil floats on top. (No oil is used as the pork must cook in its own fat. In case one does not like fatty meat, 2 tbsp of oil can be used).

4. The pork must be a little sour. Eaten after 2 or 3 days, the pandi curry is excellent. It can be preserved for a week.

# KOLI

# Koli Bartad

### INGREDIENTS

1 chicken cut into pieces

1/8 tsp turmeric

salt to taste

juice of 1 lime or vinegar or kachiyapulli

2 tsp pepper powder

1/2 tsp cumin powder

2 onions sliced

8 cloves of garlic sliced

1 piece sliced ginger

5 green chillies split into two

1/4 cup oil

1 cup water

### METHOD

1. Pour oil into a degchi. When hot, fry the onion, garlic, ginger and green chillies. Add turmeric, salt and the chicken and fry well.

2. Add water and pressure cook for 5 minutes. If gravy remains, fry till the oil comes up on top, and add lemon juice or vinegar. Serve hot..

Koli Nallamallu Fry

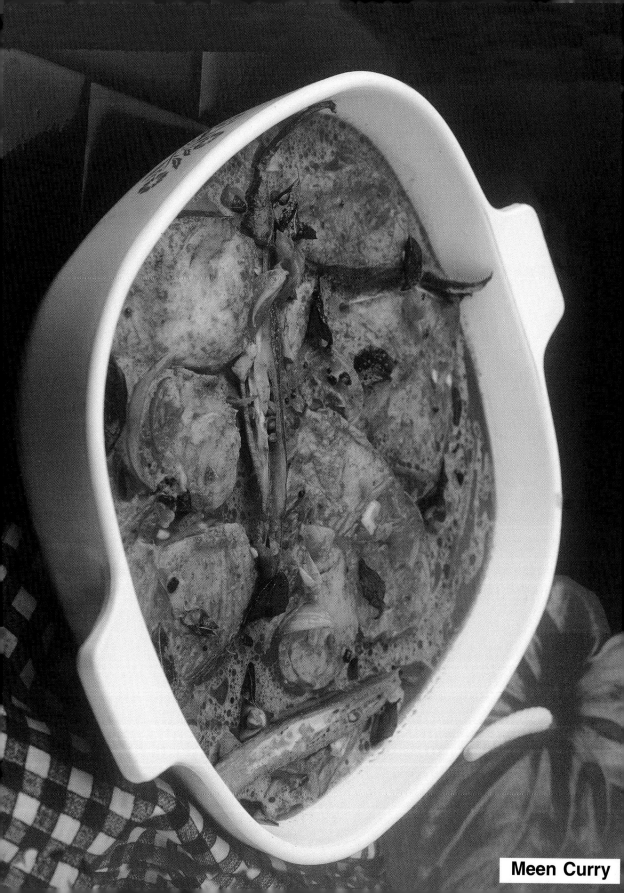

Meen Curry

# Koli Nallamallu Fry

1 chicken cut into pieces

kachiyapulli

1/4 cup oil

1 large onion sliced

salt to taste

1/4 tsp chilli powder

1 cup water

8 green chillies

1 bunch (medium) coriander leaves

1 small onion

2 tsp peppercorns

9 garlic pods

1 long piece ginger

1/4 tsp turmeric

## METHOD

1. Pour oil into a degchi. When hot, fry the sliced onion. Add the chicken and salt and water. Cook till tender. Put in the ground green masala and stir. Fry. Put in kachiyapulli (Coorg vinegar) or the juice of 1 lime.

2. Fry the chicken dry till the oil comes up on top and the chicken becomes almost black in color. Remove from heat and serve.

# Koli Curry

### INGREDIENTS

1 kg chicken cut into medium-sized pieces

1 tbsp coriander seeds

2 tsp chilli powder

1/2 tsp turmeric

the juice of 1 medium-sized lemon

1/2 tsp cumin seeds

1 piece cinnamon

4 cloves

1/2 tsp poppy seeds

salt to taste

1 medium bunch coriander leaves

1 large onion sliced

1 piece ginger

5 cloves garlic

2 cups water

1/2 cup grated coconut

1/4 cup oil

### METHOD

1. Grind the coriander seeds, chilli powder, turmeric, cumin seeds, cinnamon, cloves, garlic, ginger, poppy seeds, coriander leaves smoothly. Grind the coconut separately.

2. In a degchi, pour oil. When hot, add the onions and fry lightly. Add the ground masala, salt and fry well. When the raw smell goes, add the chicken and fry. Add water and cook till done. Add the ground coconut and gently stir. Lastly add lemon juice.

3. Remove from fire and serve hot.

# MEEN

# Meen Barthad

Any good fish with only the centre bone, or filleted into medium-sized pieces (1 kg).

### INGREDIENTS

| |
|---|
| 2 tsp chilli powder |
| 1 tsp kachiyapulli or tamarind pulp |
| 3/4 tsp salt |
| 1/2 tsp turmeric |
| 2 tbsp oil |

### METHOD

1. Mix all the above ingredients except oil with the fish till well coated. Marinate the fish for 1 hour.

2. In a flat frying pan, pour the oil. When hot, put in the fish. Lower the heat to medium, and gently fry the fish till both sides are well cooked and brown. Serve hot.

# Meen Curry

The fish used can be mackerels cut into two, or sardines. A whole raw mango (sliced) can be added with the fish.

## INGREDIENTS

1 large onion sliced

green chillies slit

1 small piece ginger

2 tbsp oil

1/8 tsp mustard seeds

1/8 tsp fenugreek seeds

salt to taste

curry leaves

1/2 cup water

1/4 cup tamarind pulp

kachiyapulli

**To grind:**

1/2 cup coconut

2 tbsp coriander seeds

1/2 tsp cumin seeds

1/4 tsp turmeric

8 cloves of garlic

1 piece ginger

Kooru Curry

Coorg Yarchi Pulav

## METHOD

1. Pour oil into a degchi. When hot put in the mustard and fenugreek seeds. Add sliced onions and fry. Add the ground masala and fry well.

2. Add salt, ginger, slit green chillies and the tamarind pulp or kachyapulli.

3. Pour water when the gravy boils. Add the fish and curry leaves.

4. Cover the degchi and cook on a medium fire. Stir well so that the fish is cooked properly. When the gravy is thick, the curry is ready. Remove from the fire and serve.

# Dry Meen and Mangai

Vegetables to be added:
Brinjal or raw banana or potatoes (sliced). As the dry fish has salt, beware of an overdose of salt to taste.

## INGREDIENTS

8 pieces of fish cut into a medium size. Roast on dry tawa, clean in fresh water to remove sand and soak for a little while in clean fresh water to remove excess salt from the fish. If raw mango is not available, grind a small lime-sized ball of tamarind.

## INGREDIENTS

| |
|---|
| *1 raw sour mango sliced* |
| *2 vegetables sliced into medium-sized pieces.* |
| *8 red dried chillies* |
| *1 tsp coriander seeds* |
| *1/2 tsp turmeric* |
| *4 cloves garlic* |
| *1 large piece ginger* |
| *6 green chillies slit at one end* |
| *1 onion sliced* |
| *1/2 cup coconut* |
| *2 tbsp oil (coconut oil preferred)* |
| *1/4 tsp mustard* |
| *1/2 cup water* |
| *Just sufficient water to cook the vegetables.* |

## METHOD

1. Grind together chillies, coriander, turmeric, garlic, ginger. Grind coconut separately.
2. Pour oil into a degchi. When hot, add mustard seeds, onion and green chillies and fry the ground masala and the coconut. Add water and the vegetables.
3. When half cooked, add the dry fish and mango. Close the lid and cook till the fish and vegetable are soft. When the gravy thickens remove from fire.

*Best eaten with white plain rice and papads.*

# Stir-fried Dry Meen

### INGREDIENTS

1 cup dried fish (washed, shredded and bones removed)
(Beware of using salt as dry fish is salty)

4 tbsp oil

1/4 tsp mustard seeds

1 sprig curry leaves

1 long piece ginger chopped

1/2 cup onions sliced

6 small green chillies chopped

1 tsp garlic crushed

salt to taste

kachiyapulli to taste

### METHOD

1. Pour oil into a pan. When smoking hot, add mustard seeds, curry leaves and all the chopped green masala. Stir for a while, add the dry fish and sprinkle a little water. When cooked well and roasted, remove from fire and serve hot.

# Meen Cutlet

### INGREDIENTS

*1 cup fish cooked with salt and vinegar and mashed roughly*

*1/2 cup potato cooked and mashed*

*2 tbsp oil*

*1/4 cup finely chopped onion*

*5 green chillies finely chopped*

*1 large piece ginger finely chopped*

*small sprigs of mint and coriander leaves chopped finely*

*vinegar to taste or lemon juice*

*salt to taste*

*1 egg*

*breadcrumbs.*

### METHOD

1. Put in a little oil in a frying pan. When hot add onions, green chillies, ginger and fry a little. Add the mashed fish, vinegar and salt, and remove from the fire after stirring it well. Add lemon juice.

2. When cold, add the mashed potatoes and the egg yolk. Mix well and add the coriander and minced mint leaves

3. Make medium-sized balls and flatten them into any desired shape. Dip each of the cutlets in the whisked egg white and roll them in breadcrumbs.

4. With the remaining oil fry the cutlets in a flat frying pan to a golden brown.

*Cutlets can be kept in a sealed container in the refrigerator without frying. Fry as and when required.*

# TARAKARI

# Belai Curry

### INGREDIENTS

*1/2 cup tuvar dal washed and soaked*

*1 big onion sliced*

*2 large green or ripe tomatoes*

*a few beans cut into four pieces*

*salt to taste*

*1/2 tsp cumin powder*

*1 tsp coriander powder*

*1/2 tsp red chilli powder*

*1/4 tsp mustard seeds*

*1 tbsp oil*

*1 tbsp jaggery*

*1/4 tsp turmeric powder*

*1 cup water*

### METHOD

1. Pressure cook dal with turmeric for seven minutes in water (1 cup)
2. In a degchi heat the oil and fry the mustard seeds, the masala powder, salt, raw tomatoes and beans
3. Fry the contents for sometime. When cooked, add the dal. If the gravy is a little too thick add more water. Lastly add jaggery. Serve with rice.

# Kooru Curry

### INGREDIENTS

1/2 cup rajma soaked overnight

1/2 cup green beans broken into three pieces

1 onion chopped

8 cloves of garlic chopped

1/2 tsp chilli powder

1 tsp coriander powder

1/2 cup coconut (ground)

1/4 tsp turmeric powder

1/4 tsp cumin powder

1 tbsp tamarind ground

11/2 cup water

salt to taste

1/4 tsp sugar

a few red chillies for seasoning

1 tbsp oil

curry leaves

1/4 tsp mustard seeds

### METHOD

1. Cook the rajma well. Put in the cooked beans.
2. In a degchi, pour the oil, when hot add mustard seeds, garlic, curry leaves, onion and fry. Add the balance masala and fry. Add the rajma and boil, adding coconut paste mixed with water (so as to not form lumps). Add sugar.
3. Mix everything well and serve.

# Ripe Mangai Paji

## INGREDIENTS

6 ripe mangoes

**To grind:**

1/2 cup coconut. (grated)

4 green chillies

6 cloves of garlic

1/2 tsp mustard seeds

**To keep aside:**

2 cups beaten curd

salt to taste

1 tsp sugar

1 tbsp oil

2 cups water

## METHOD

1. Peel the ripe mango and keep aside.
2. In a degchi, pour oil and put in mustard. Fry the ground masala and coconut. Add 2 cups of water, salt and sugar.
3. Put in the beaten curd and mangoes and stir. Do not overheat or boil.
4. If people do not like curds, leave the curd out of the chutney/curry.

*Best eaten with ghee rice (naikulu) or Coorg biriyani.*

# Fried Cauliflower

*1 large cauliflower cut into large florets*

*salt to taste*

**To grind:**

*1/4 tsp turmeric powder*

*6 green chillies (ground)*

*1 medium bunch coriander leaves*

*1 onion*

*2 tbsp maida*

*1 egg*

*1 cup oil*

## METHOD

1. Boil the cauliflower in salt and turmeric. Throw the water away and strain.
2. Mix the maida, salt, egg, ground chilies and coriander leaves into a smooth paste.
3. Coat the cauliflower florets with this paste..
4. In a wok pour oil. When hot fry the cauliflower till golden and crisp.
5. Serve hot.

# Chakai Curry

Small, unripe, tender jackfruit, peeled, cleaned and chopped into small pieces (cubes). Wash well.
1/4 cup rajma soaked and cooked.

## INGREDIENTS

| |
|---|
| 1/2 tsp turmeric powder |
| salt to taste |
| 1/4 tsp mustard seeds |
| 3 cups water |
| 2 tsp coriander powder |
| 1 tsp chilli powder |
| 1/2 tsp cumin powder |
| 8 cloves of garlic pounded |
| 1 big onion |
| 1/2 cup ground coconut |
| 2 tbsp oil |

## METHOD

1. Pressure cook unripe jackfruit in 3 cups of water with turmeric and salt till medium tender, for 5 minutes. Keep aside.

2. In a degchi, pour oil and season with mustard, pounded garlic and onion.

3. After the mixture has turned brown, add the dry masala powders and the coconut paste and fry just a little. Add the cooked rajma and the jackfruit and boil for about 2 minutes.

4. Remove from fire.

*Best eaten with akki ooti, rice chappatis.*

# Chakai Fry

Small, unripe, tender jackfruit, peeled, cleaned and cut into big pieces.

### INGREDIENTS

| |
|---|
| *1/4 tsp turmeric powder* |
| *salt to taste* |
| *4 green chillies slit into 4 pieces each* |
| *2 onions cut into long slices* |
| *1/2 tsp lemon juice* |
| *1/2 tsp mustard seeds* |
| *2 tbsp oil* |
| *3 cups water* |
| *1 tsp coriander power* |
| *1/2 tsp cumin powder* |
| *1/2 cup coconut (grated)* |

### METHOD

1. Pour oil into a degchi. Season with mustard seeds, add onions and fry.
2. Put in the slit green chillies, add the shredded unripe jackfruit. Add salt to taste.
3. Add lime juice and stir fry without breaking the fruit.
4. Add the coriander and cumin powders.
5. Mix in the coconut and remove from the fire.
6. Serve hot.

# Raw Mangai Curry

6 unripe mangoes cut into 4 pieces each, with skin and matured seed.

### INGREDIENTS

| | |
|---|---|
| | 2 cups water |
| **To grind:** | |
| | 1 tsp cumin seeds |
| | 1 large onion |
| | 3 green chillies |
| | salt to taste |
| | 1 tsp chilli powder |
| | 1 tsp mustard seeds |
| | (1/2 of the mustard seeds to be roasted and powdered and kept aside.) |
| | 2 tbsp coriander powder |
| | 1/2 tsp turmeric |
| | 1/2 cup powdered jaggery |
| | 8 cloves of garlic sliced |

### METHOD

1. Pour oil into a degchi, fry mustard seeds and garlic till they turn brown.
2. Add ground masala and dry masala and fry lightly, Add salt and the cut mango pieces. Add water and jaggery.
3. Cook till the outer part of the mango is cooked. The consistency of the curry should be syrupy.
4. Add the roasted mustard powder and stir. Remove from the fire.

*This curry can be preserved for over a week.*

# Tarakari Curry

6 beans

3 potatoes

2 carrots

8 florets of cauliflower (medium size)

1/2 cup peas

**To grind:**

3 green chillies

1/2 tsp cumin powder

1 tbsp coriander seeds

1/2 cup coconut

4 dry red chillies

1 tbsp tamarind

1 tbsp oil

1/4 tsp mustard feeds

salt to taste

2 cups water

3 cloves of garlic pounded

1 large onion

## METHOD

1. Heat a degchi, add oil and put in the mustard seeds. Fry with garlic and onion to a brown colour.
2. Add the ground masala and fry.
3. Put in the cleaned and cut vegetables. Add water and salt to taste.
4. When cooked add tamarind paste.
5. Serve hot.

# Kaipaikai Curry

Clean the bitter gourd and chop into thin pieces. Wash and mix with salt and keep it aside for 1 hour. Afterwards squeeze the bitter gourd to remove the bitter taste.

### INGREDIENTS

1 large onion cut into long pieces

1/4 cup oil

salt to taste

1/2 cup jaggery

1/4 tsp mustard seeds

2 tsp coriander powder

1 tsp cumin powder

1 tsp red chilli powder

1/2 tsp turmeric

4 green chillies slit long

6 cloves of garlic minced

2 inch piece ginger minced

1/2 cup tamarind pulp

### METHOD

1. In a degchi pour oil. When hot put the mustard seeds, green chillies, sliced onions, minced garlic, ginger, and fry.

2. Add the powder masala and salt and fry the bitter gourd well. Add water, close lid and cook.

3. When medium soft add tamarind pulp and more salt. Allow to cook.

4. When soft, add jaggery and little water, and stir till it is dry.

# Moodaray Kanee

## INGREDIENTS

1 kg horse gram (cleaned)

lots of water

1 tbsp cumin powder

1 tbsp mustard powder

1 tbsp khus khus

1 tbsp black pepper

10 red dry chillies

8 green chillies

(Grind the above masala, after roasting it lightly, into powder)

1/4 cup oil

**To grind:**

1 inch piece ginger

1 clove of garlic

1 onion

salt to taste

1/4 cup jaggery

1/4 cup tamarind pulp

2 sprigs of curry leaves

## METHOD

1. Pressure cook the horse gram for over an hour till the gram is cooked.
2. Drain it and grind a cup of cooked horse gram and keep it aside.
3. The drained juice and the ground dal should be mixed properly. The mixture should not be watery, but medium thick.

4. In a degchi, pour oil, add curry leaves. When hot put in the garlic, ginger, onion and the drained dal water mixture...

5. Add salt and jaggery and cook till it boils.

6. Add tamarind and then the roasted masala powder. Allow to thicken into a sauce-like mixture.

7. Remove from fire and preserve in a bottle. To be eaten with rice or akki ooti.

**Muttai Curry With Potatoes**

Thindi

# Koomu Curry

Clean and cut the end of each stalk and cut the mushroom into two. In Coorg, we get wild mushroom which are edible and the taste is entirely different from that of the cultivated variety. The oyster mushroom gives a wild mushroom taste. Round button mushrooms are good for pickles or for pepper onion fry.

### INGREDIENTS

2 pkts washed, cleaned and cut mushrooms

6 green chillies split and kept aside

**To grind:**

1 tbsp coriander seeds

1/2 tsp cumin seeds

6 cloves garlic

1/4 tsp turmeric

1/2 tsp peppercorns

4 dry red chillies

1/4 cup oil

1 large onion sliced lengthwise

1 large or 2 small tomatoes (chopped)

a small bunch of coriander leaves finely chopped

2 sprigs of curry leaves

1/2 cup water

salt to taste

juice of 1/2 lemon

**Koottu Curry**

## METHOD

1. In a degchi, pour oil, put in the onions, curry leaves, slit green chillies and saute.
2. Add the ground masala and fry well.
3. Put in the coconut after making it into a paste.
4. Add water and salt to taste.
5. Add the mushrooms and tomatoes and cook on a slow fire till they are cooked.
6. The gravy should not be thin or thick. Add the coriander leaves and the lemon juice.
7. Serve hot.

# Koomu Barthad

Clean, cut and wash the button mushrooms.

## INGREDIENTS

2 onions sliced

8 cloves garlic sliced

8 green chillies slit and cut lengthwise

1 tsp pepper powder

salt to taste

1/4 cup water

1 tbsp lime juice

1/4 cup oil

## METHOD

1. In a degchi, pour oil and when hot, saute the onions and garlic till they turn a golden brown. Add green chillies, mushroom and pepper powder and stir fry. Add water and cook on a slow fire. When ready, add lime juice and serve hot.

# Tomato Curry

## INGREDIENTS

6 tomatoes cut into pieces

4 cloves of garlic

1 large onion

1 1/2 cups water

salt to taste

4 green chillies

2 tsp chilli powder

1 tsp coriander seeds

1/2 tsp mustard seeds

3/4 tsp fenugreek seeds

1 tbsp tamarind

2 1/2 tsp jaggery grated

2 tbsp oil

## METHOD

1. Fry the dry masala on a low fire. Do not let it discolour. Grind it well.

2. Pour oil in a vessel and when it splatters add mustard and fenugreek seeds. Add the ground masala, turmeric, chilli powder, the cut green chillies. Add tomatoes. Mix the tamarind pulp and enough salt to taste and 1 1/2 cups water. Allow to boil, then simmer on a gentle fire. When medium cooked, add the jaggery and take it off the fire. Never overcook the tomotoes.

# Beans Fried

## INGREDIENTS

1 cup full of beans cut into small pieces or lengthwise

1 large onion sliced lengthwise

4 green chillies slit into two

1/4 tsp mustard seeds

2 tbsp oil

3 tbsp grated coconut

1/2 cup water

salt to taste

## METHOD

1. In a degchi, put in the oil. When hot, add the mustard seeds, onion, green chillies, vegetable and salt. Add water and cook the beans.

2. Remove from fire and sprinkle grated coconut over it.

3. Serve hot.

# BAMBOO SHOOT PREPARATIONS

# Bamboo Curry

4 cups of chopped bamboo shoots cooked in 1/4 tsp turmeric and salt till tender. 5 cups of water.

### INGREDIENTS

*1 onion sliced*

*4 green chillies sliced lengthwise*

*4 cloves of garlic pounded and kept aside*

**To grind:**

*1/2 cup coconut grated*

*1/2 tsp mustard seeds*

*1 tsp red chilli powder*

*1/2 tsp cumin powder*

*1/2 tsp pepper powder*

*2 tsp coriander powder*

*1/2 cup water*

*salt to taste*

### METHOD

1.  Heat degchi with oil, add onion, mustard and garlic, and fry till brown. Put in all the masala and the green chilli and fry. Add the bamboo shoots and pour in the rest of the water. Add salt to taste. Cook the curry till it boils and remove from fire. Serve hot.

# Fried Bamboo Shoots

4 cups of chopped bamboo shoots cooked in 1/4 tsp turmeric and salt till tender. 5 cups of water.

### INGREDIENTS

2 cups bamboo shoots (cooled)

**For roasting:**

1/2 tsp mustard seeds

1/2 tsp cumin seeds

1 tbsp uncooked rice

1 tsp peppercorns

**To keep aside:**

1 onion sliced

1 clove garlic sliced

1/4 tsp mustard powder

4 green chillies sliced

1 tbsp oil

1/2 cup water

salt to taste

1 tbsp lemon juice

### METHOD

1. In a degchi pour in oil. When hot, add mustard seeds, onions and garlic. Let it turn brown, stirring all the time. Add green chilli, and then the bamboo shoots, and fry well. Then add the roasted masala and a little water to keep it moist. Add lemon juice. Serve hot.

# Kay-Boo-Curry

Patarvel (yam leaves) curry.
Only the edible kind of patarvel can be used, otherwise the whole mouth itches. Pluck only the tender leaves with tender stems. Clean and devein the leaves. The stem can be cut into small pieces and can also be used.

### INGREDIENTS

| |
|---|
| 1/2 cup tuvar dal |
| 1 1/2 cup water |
| 6 large patarvel leaves |
| salt to taste |
| 1/4 tsp mustard seeds |
| 4 green chillies |
| 1 tsp cumin seeds |
| 11/2 tsp coriander seeds |
| 2 tbsp tamarind |
| 10 cloves garlic |
| 1 large onion |
| 3 red chillies (dry) |
| 1/4 tsp turmeric powder |
| 11/2 tbsp oil |

### METHOD

1. Chop the leaves finely.
2. Cook tuvar dal separately. Boil the patarvel in water with salt.
3. After it is cooked take a ladle and mash the leaves or put in the liquidiser.
4. Grind the coriander seeds, cumin seeds, green chillies, tamarind, turmeric and cloves of garlic.
5. Pour oil in a vessel. When hot put in mustard seeds, dry red chillies, pounded garlic and onion, and on a slow fire, add the ground masala and the mashed patarvel leaves and dal. Stir fry well and add salt to taste. When the curry becomes thick, remove from fire and serve.

# Pachai Mallu Curry

*1 cup slit green chillies (remove the seeds). Chop finely and soak in cold water for 15 minutes and remove.*

*Chop an equal amount of onions finely*

**To grind:**

*2 large onions*

*1 tsp cumin seeds*

*1/2 cup coconut(optional)*

*1/4 tsp turmeric*

*salt to taste*

*1/2 cup oil*

*1/4 tsp mustard seeds*

*5 cloves garlic*

*2 sprigs curry leaves*

*3/4 cup tamarind pulp*

*1/2 cup jaggery (according to taste)*

*1 cup water*

## METHOD

1. Mix chillies, onion, the chopped and ground masala, salt and turmeric.

2. In a vessel, pour 1/3 cup of oil, and when it is hot put in the mustard, a few cloves of garlic and curry leaves.

3. Add the chilli mixture and 1 cup water and cook the mixture on a slow fire. When the mixture is cooked, add tamarind pulp, more salt and jaggery. Remove from fire. Chilli curry will taste hot, sweet, and sour, and taste delicious with plain white rice with fried fish or dry chicken or mutton.

# YARCHI

# Pooyarchi Bartad

### INGREDIENTS

1/2 kg liver sliced

1 cup onions sliced

2 tsp pepper powder

6 green chillis slit

8 cloves garlic sliced

2 inch piece ginger sliced

1 medium bunch coriander leaves

1/4 tsp turmeric powder

salt to taste

1/4 cup oil

1/2 cup water

### METHOD

1. Pour oil into a degchi and when hot add onions, green chilli, garlic, ginger, coriander leaves, turmeric, salt to taste and add the sliced liver. Fry well. Add 1/2 cup of water and cook on a slow fire. Cook the liver till the oil floats on top.

# Yarchi Brain Fried

## INGREDIENTS

4 brains

Soak the brains in salted water for some time. Clean it well.

**Keep aside:**

1 large onion sliced

1/2 cup water

1/4 cup oil

juice of 1 medium-sized lemon

3 green chillies slit into four pieces

salt to taste

**To grind:**

8 green chillies

1/2 tsp peppercorns

1 medium bunch coriander leaves

8 garlic cloves chopped

1 small piece ginger

3 cloves

1 piece cinnamon

## METHOD

1. In a flat frying pan pour oil, and when hot, fry the sliced onions.
2. Meanwhile mix the ground masala and salt with the brains.
3. When the onion is lightly fried, add the brain masala and saute it carefully.
4. Pour water when the masala is well fried, cover it and cook on a slow fire.
5. Lastly add green chillies and the lemon juice and more salt if required.

*Never break the single brain.*

Serve on a platter.

# Kyma Unday

## INGREDIENTS

1/2 kg mutton minced

**To grind:**

1 piece ginger

8 cloves of garlic

1 medium bunch coriander leaves

1 tsp peppercorns

6 green chillies

1 large onion

1 tbsp. tamarind

1 piece cinnamon

4 cloves

1/4 tsp turmeric powder

1/4 cup puffed Bengal gram

salt to taste

## METHOD

1. Mix the mince mutton with the ground masala and make into small-sized balls
2. In a vessel pour 1 cup of water and add the curry leaves. When the water boils add the mince balls. Allow to cook till the water evaporates or steam it.
3. When cool, keep in a closed container.
4. Whenever you require it, fry it till brown in 1 tbsp ghee..

# Yarchi Curry

*1/2 kg mutton cleaned and cut into medium size pieces with bones*

*1/2 tsp turmeric powder*

*1 tsp chilli powder*

*salt to taste*

**METHOD**

1. Mix the mutton with the above masala and keep it aside for half an hour. Pressure cook the meat for 20 minutes.

**INGREDIENTS TO GRIND:**

*1/2 cup coconut ground separately*

*1 medium bunch coriander leaves*

*11/2 tsp coriander seeds*

*1 tsp khus khus*

*4 cloves*

*1 piece cinnamon*

*1 inch piece ginger*

*8 pods garlic*

*1 large onion sliced*

*1/4 cup oil*

*4 cups water*

*1 large tomato (chopped)*

*juice of 1 lemon*

## Method

1. In a vessel pour oil, When the oil becomes hot fry the onions to a golden colour. Add ground masala and fry.
2. When half fried, add the chopped tomatoes and fry till the oil floats on top of the masala.
3. Add the cooked meat and the ground coconut.
4. The gravy should cover the meat.
5. Lastly add the lemon juice and stir.
6. Eat with rice ghee rice or any puttus.

# Yarchi Nallamallu Bartad

### INGREDIENTS

1/2 kg mutton cut into medium-sized pieces, cleaned and washed. (Rub turmeric and salt and keep it aside.)

1 cup baby onions(sambar onions)

1 tsp pepper (powdered)

1/2 tsp cumin powder

8 pods garlic sliced

1 piece ginger sliced

1/4 cup oil

4 cups water

### METHOD

1. Pour oil into a degchi and when hot lightly fry the onion (saute only.)

2. Add garlic and ginger, fry a little, add pepper, cummin and the mutton. Fry it well adding a little water from time to time.

3. When fried, add the balance water and pressure cook for 20 minutes, till the mutton is well cooked. Remove lid and keep frying till dry.

# Kodagu Yarchi Bartad

1 kg mutton with bones—cut into medium pieces.

## INGREDIENTS

**To grind:**

*6 red chillies*

*1/2 tsp peppercorns*

*11/2 tsp coriander seeds*

*1/2 tsp turmeric*

*1/2 tsp cumin seeds*

*1 piece cinnamon*

*2 cardamoms*

*4 cloves*

*1/4 cup oil*

*3 onions sliced*

*1 piece ginger thinly sliced*

*5 cups water*

*salt to taste*

*Broil on hot greased skillet*

## METHOD

1. Mix the masala with the mutton pieces. Marinate for 1 hour.
2. In a pressure cooker cook the mutton with water fro 20 minutes. Dry all the gravy.
3. In a vessel, heat the oil, fry the sliced onions, garlic and ginger.
4. Add the cooked mutton and keep stir frying till it is dark brown in colour and the gravy sticks to the mutton.
5. Serve hot.

# Yarchi Chops

1 kg double chops flattened.

## INGREDIENTS

**To grind:**

4 cloves

2 inch piece cinnamon

juice of 1 lemon

6 green chillies

6 cloves of garlic

1 1/2 piece ginger

1 tsp peppercorns

1 medium bunch coriander leaves

1/2 tsp turmeric

6 cups water

1/2 cup cooking oil

salt to taste

Mix the chops with the ground masala and keep aside for 1 hour.

## METHOD

1. Put the pressure cooker on the stove. Pour in oil. When hot add the chops and fry well. Keep adding a little water at a time while frying. Add all the water and pressure cook it for 20 minutes.

2. Stir fry the chops gently without breaking them.

3. Arrange on a platter and serve.

# Kodagu Cutlets

### INGREDIENTS

1 cup minced meat

8 tbsp oil

1/4 cup minced onion

4 green chillies minced

1 bunch green coriander minced

salt to taste

1/2 tsp pepper powder

1/4 tsp chilli powder

1/2 lime lemon juice

1/2 cup mashed potato

1 egg

breadcrumbs

1/2 cup water

### METHOD

1. In a degchi, pour some oil. When the oil becomes hot, fry the onion, green chillies, chilli powder and pepper. Add the mince meat and salt . Add 1/2 cup of water. Cook it till the mutton becomes tender.

2. Cool the meat and add the coriander leaves and lime juice. Mix in the mashed potatoes and the egg yolk.

3. Flatten into cutlets of desired shapes. Whisk the egg white. Dip the cutlet one by one into the egg white and then roll in the breadcrumbs.

4. Fry them in shallow oil and serve.

# Yarchi Stew

Eaten with paputtu or noolputtu

### INGREDIENTS

*1/2 kg mutton cut into medium-sized pieces (with bones).*

*juice of 1/2 lemon*

*salt to taste*

*1 tbsp ghee*

*1/2 cup sliced onion*

*6 green chillies slit*

*1/2 tsp ginger sliced*

*6 cloves of garlic*

*1/2 tsp crushed pepper*

*3 pieces cinnamons*

*6 cloves*

*2 cardamom*

*2 sprigs curry leaves*

*3 potatoes cut into 4 pieces each*

*1/2 cup thick coconut milk*

*2 cups thin coconut milk*

*1 tbsp maida flour*

*1 tbsp ghee*

### METHOD

1.  In a degchi put in the thin coconut milk and add all the spices, and lastly add the meat.
2.  Pressure cook the meat for 20 minutes on a medium fire. Add salt .

3.  When the meat is done, add the maida paste and cook till the gravy is thick.

4.  Add the lime juice, the cooked potatoes and the ghee.

5.  Simmer. Add the thick coconut milk and remove from fire.

*If desired, medium-sized whole onions can be added and cooked with the meat when it is 3/4th done.*

# Kyma Curry

INGREDIENTS

**To grind:**

1/2 kg minced meat

1 large onion minced

1/2 tsp minced green chilli

1/2 tsp minced ginger

1/2 tsp minced garlic

3 tsp coriander seeds

5 red chillies

1/2 tsp turmeric

1/4 tsp cumin seeds

3 cloves

1 piece cinnamon

1 egg

**Keep aside:**

half of the ground masala

1 onion sliced

4 slit green chillies

1/2 cup thick coconut milk

1/2 cup thin coconut milk

1/4 cup oil

2 sprigs curry leaves

## METHOD

1.  Mix the minced meat with half the quantity of ground masala and one egg, and form into medium-sized balls. Keep aside.

2.  In a vessel, pour the oil, and when hot, fry the onion, green chilli, curry leaves and the remaining half of the ground masala.

3.  Add the thin coconut milk and drop the meat balls one by one into the gravy. When half cooked, gently, without breaking them, turn the balls around. When the meat balls are done, add the thick coconut milk.

4.  Swirl them around and remove from the fire. Never allow the thick coconut milk to boil. It should remain thick.

5.  Serve hot.

# Nad Muttai Omelette

## INGREDIENTS

4 chicken eggs

1/2 cup cooked rice made into a paste

1 large onion finely chopped

4 green chillies finely chopped

1 medium bunch green coriander finely chopped

salt to taste

3 tbsp oil

## METHOD

1. Beat the eggs till fluffy. Add salt and the ground rice and make into a smooth mixture. Add chopped onions, green chillies and coriander leaves.

2. Pour oil onto a tawa. When hot, pour in the beaten egg to make a simple omelette.

3. Tune the heat to low till one side is golden in colour. Then brown the other side. Do not fold the omelette. It should be round.

# Egg Curry With Potatoes

### INGREDIENTS

*6 eggs hard boiled, (shelled and halved)*

*potatoes cut into cubes*

*1/4 tsp turmeric*

*1 large ginger sliced*

*4 garlic pods sliced*

*4 green chillies halved*

*salt to taste*

*4 dry red chillies*

*1/2 tsp peppercorns*

*2 tsp coriander seeds*

*1/4 tsp cumin seeds*

*1 piece cinnamon broken into 4 pieces*

*4 cloves*

*2 cardamoms*

*1/4 cup oil*

*1/2 cup grated coconut*

*1 tsp lemon juice*

*1 sprig of curry leaves.*

### METHOD

1. Broil the chillies, coriander seeds, cumin, pepper, turmeric in a greased skillet, Grind them together. Grind the coconut separately.

2. Pour oil into a degchi. When hot, add the sliced onion, garlic, ginger and green chillies. Add the ground masala and fry well.

3. Pour in water, add the ground coconut, potatoes, and salt to taste.

4. When the potatoes are nearly done, carefully add the eggs.

5. The gravy should cover the eggs. Add lemon juice and remove from fire.

6. Serve hot.

# DESSERTS

## Albai

### INGREDIENTS

| |
|---|
| 1/2 coconut grated |
| 1 cup rice soaked and ground |
| 2 cardamoms powdered |
| salt to taste |
| 1/2 cup sugar |
| 2 tbsp ghee |

### METHOD

1. In a muslin cloth sieve the ground rice,
2. Add salt and sugar to taste.
3. In a wok on the fire, keep on stirring the mixture.
4. When it thickens to a halwa-like consistency, spread it on a thali or flat plate, adding a little ghee to it.
5. Cut into pieces when cool.

# Vermicelli Payasa

## Ingredients

1 cup vermicelli, lightly fried on a hot skillet greased with ghee

2 cups water

2 cups fresh thick milk

or

tinned milk

1 tbsp sugar

1 pinch saffron

1/2 tsp cardamom powder

1 tbsp cashewnuts fried and chopped

1/2 tsp raisins (fried)

3 tbsp ghee

## Method

1. Add the vermicelli to the boiling water and cook.
2. When it is half done, add milk and stir continuously.
3. Add sugar, saffron, cardamom powder, cashewnuts, raisins and ghee.
4. Remove from fire and serve.

# Baleya Murukk

### INGREDIENTS

1 cup mashed ripe bananas

3/4 cup maida flour

2 tbsp sugar

1/4 cup water

1/2 cup milk

salt to taste

1/4 tsp soda bicarb

1 cup oil

### METHOD

1. Mix the flour, banana, sugar, water, milk, salt and soda bicarb into a rather thickish batter.

2. In a wok, add the oil and when hot, pour 1 tsp of the batter into the oil. Lower the fire and cook till till the mixture becomes blackish brown.

3. Drain the baleya murukk and keep doing the same with the balance batter.

4. Serve hot.

# Kolai Puttu

With ripe banana or jackfruit wrapped in banana leaf

### INGREDIENTS

*8 ripe bananas (mashed)*

*2 cups brokens rice (thari)*

*3 cardamoms powdered*

*1/2 cup sugar*

*2 tbsp ghee*

*a little water*

*1 large green banana leaf cut into squares*

### METHOD

1. Mix the mashed banana and broken rice, sugar, cardamom powder and ghee together to form a thick paste, adding a little water.

2. Take a large banana leaf. Cut the leaf into large squares and warm the pieces over the fire, so that they become soft and tender.

3. Pour on it 1 1/2 tbsp of the mixture, flatten it and fold the leaf into a packet. Repeat the process.

4. Cook on a steam cooker. Remove the leaves when done and eat the kolai puttu with thick ghee.

# Kul Kul

## INGREDIENTS

4 cups maida

2 eggs

1 cup sugar

1 tsp butter

11/2 cup oil

1/2 cup thick coconut mulk

pinch of salt

1/2 cup sugar

## METHOD

1. Mix butter and eggs. Add flour, salt, coconut milk, half of the sugar and butter. Knead into a dough.

2. Make little flat rounds. Press the end of the fork into them. Fry in deep oil.

3. Make a syrup by boiling 1/2 cup sugar with 1 cup water. Remove from fire.

4. Mix fried kulkul in the syrup for a coating of sugar.

5. It need not be coated with sugar and can just be eaten plain.

# Baley Halwa

## INGREDIENTS

*12 overripe peeled boiled, cored and mashed bananas*

*2 cups sugar*

*1 cup ghee*

## METHOD

1. Mix the mashed banana and sugar in a large heavy skillet, and on a medium fire stir continuously till the banana sticks to the skillet. Keep stirring. Add the ghee. The ghee will begin to ooze out from the banana pulp. Keep stirring all the time.

2. Remove from fire and spread the halwa on a greased plate evenly, with the back of a ladle to make the surface smooth and even.

3. Cut into pieces and serve.

# THINDI

# Mutton Puffs

### INGREDIENTS

1/4 kg mutton minced and cooked

4 potatoes cut into small pieces

2 tsp ground chillies

1 tsp coriander powder

3 pods of garlic chopped finely

juice of 1/2 lime

3 onions sliced

1/4" piece ginger chopped

4 green chillies chopped

1 tsp coriander leaves chopped

1/2 tsp cumin powder

1/2 tsp turmeric

salt to taste

2 cups oil

### METHOD

1. Fry the onions, chilli, and the masala. Add the cooked minced meat and dry it on the fire.

**To make dough:**

| |
|---|
| *11/2 cups maida* |
| *a little salt* |
| *2 tbsp butter or dalda* |
| *a little water* |
| *1/4 tsp baking soda* |

**METHOD**

1. Knead the mixture well into a soft dough.
2. Close the puff into a cone, using water to stick.
3. With a fork mark the sealed puffs.
4. Deep fry to a golden brown.
5. Serve hot.

# Diamond Cut

### INGREDIENTS

*2 cups maida flour*

*2 eggs*

*4 tbsp ghee*

*pinch of salt*

*11/2 cups oil*

*1/2 cup sugar*

*3/4 cup thick coconut milk*

### METHOD

1. Sift the flour, add 4 tbsp of ghee into it, mix well. Break the eggs into it, add salt, sugar and the thick coconut milk, to make into a dough.

2. Roll out on a floured board and cut into diamond shapes.

3. Fry in hot oil and when light golden in colour, remove them from the fire.

4. When cool, store them in a tin.

# Karjeekai

## INGREDIENTS

1 cup suji

11/2 cups maida flour

100 gms cashewnuts powdered

11/2 cups sugar powdered

1 cup dry copra grated

1/2 tsp cardamom

3 tbsp ghee

1 tbsp khus khus

2 tbsp raisins

11/2 cups oil for frying.

## METHOD

1. In a kadai, over moderate heat, fry the suji to a light brown colour.
2. In a little ghee fry the cashewnuts, raisins, cardamom, copra and khus khus till it is light brown in colour.
3. Remove from fire, add sugar and mix well. Keep the stuffing aside.
4. Make a soft dough of the suji and maida flour, adding the ghee to it.
5. Roll each ball into small puris and fill with the stuffing. Close each puff with water and firmly seal them.
6. Heat oil in the kadai and fry the puffs in batches, to a soft golden brown colour, turning it gently in the oil.
7. Keep the puffs in airtight tins or plastic containers for a fortnight.

# PAJI

# Kodagu Paji

Coconut and sesame chutney to be eaten with akki ooti.

### INGREDIENTS

**To grind:**

| |
|---|
| *2 tbsp sesame seeds, lightly roasted on the tawa.* |
| *1/2 cup grated coconut* |
| *1 tbsp tamarind pulp* |
| *2 green chillies* |
| *11/2 tsp jaggery* |
| *salt to taste* |
| *water to grind* |

### METHOD

1. Grind into a semi-thick paste. Do not season.
2. Mix with hot ghee and eat it for breakfast with akki ooti.

# Coconut Paji

To eat with any meal or ootis.

## INGREDIENTS

**To grind:**

1/2 cup grated coconut

3 green chillies

salt to taste

1 tsp oil

1 tbsp tamarind pulp

1/2 an onion

1/8 tsp mustard seeds

## METHOD

1. Grind roughly and season with mustard in hot oil. Add a little water and remove from fire.

# Citron Curd Paji

Peel the citron as you would an orange and remove the segments. Deseed and keep it aside.

## INGREDIENTS

**To grind:**

4 green chillies

1/2 tbsp lime juice

salt to taste

1/2 cup grated coconut

4 garlic cloves

1 tsp mustard seeds

1/2 tsp cumin powder

1/2 tsp sugar

Add these with the citron segments.

**For seasoning:**

1 tbsp oil

1/8 tsp mustard seeds

1 sprig curry leaves

4 pounded garlic cloves

1/2 onion chopped

2 dry red chillies broken to pieces

2 cups thick curd.

## METHOD

1.  In a degchi add oil. When hot, add the seasoning and fry till brown in colour. Pour in the chutney and stir. Add the curd, salt and the sugar.

2.  Remove from fire.

# Citron Paji

2 large citrons, to be roasted on fire till almost blackish in colour. Remove the black peel and the seeds

### INGREDIENTS

4 dry red chillies (roasted)

1 full garlic (peeled)

1/2 onion chopped

1 tbsp jaggery

salt to taste

1/8 tsp mustard seeds

1 tbsp tamarind

**For the seasoning:**

1/2 cup oil

1/8 tsp mustard seeds

1 sprig curry leaves

3 cloves of garlic pounded

2 dry red chillies broken

### METHOD

1. Grind the citrons, garlic, tamarind, roasted red chilli, jaggery and salt.
2. Pour 1/2 cup oil into a degchi. When hot, add mustard seeds, curry leaves, red dry chillies and garlic, Add the chutney and keep frying well till it turns into a reddish colour. The oil should float on the top.
3. When cold, store it in a bottle. Can be kept for almost a year.

# Cucumber Paji

## INGREDIENTS

*1 large cucumber roughly pounded and ground*

*4 green chillies*

*1/4 cup coconut*

*salt to taste*

*1 tbsp lime juice*

*1/8 tsp mustard seeds*

*1 sprig curry leaves*

*1 onion chopped finely*

*6 cloves of garlic pounded*

*11/2 tsp oil*

*1 cup beaten curd*

## METHOD

1. Grind the green chilli, coconut, salt, and add the roughly ground cucumber. Beat the curd.

2. Season with hot oil, mustard seeds, pounded garlic and onion. Mix the cucumber chutney with the beaten curd. Add salt.

3. Serve with biriyani or akki ooti, or kadambuttu, as breakfast dishes.

# Ginger Paji

INGREDIENTS

4 cloves of garlic pounded

1 large piece ginger cleaned and peeled

1/2 cup coconut scraped

4 green chillies

4 cloves of garlic

1 large onion

1 medium bunch coriander leaves

salt to taste

1 cup beaten curd

water as required

11/2 tsp oil for seasoning

1/4 tsp mustard seeds

## METHOD

1. Grind all the green masala with the coconut and salt. Add water and grind smoothly.
2. Fry mustard seeds and pounded garlic in oil and add the chutney to it.
3. Remove from fire, add the beaten curd and stir well.
4. Eat with Coorg biriyani or ghee rice.

# Horse Gram and Coconut Paji

### INGREDIENTS

*1/4 cup roasted horse gram*

*1 tbsp tamarind pulp*

*salt to taste*

*3 green chillies*

*2 cloves garlic*

*1/8 tsp mustard seeds*

*1/2 onion chopped*

*1 sprig curry leaves*

*water as required*

*1 tsp oil*

### METHOD

1. Grind the horse gram roughly and remove the skin in a seive, Put it in a little water and allow it to soak for a quarter of an hour.

2. Remove and grind the horse gram, green chillies, salt, tamarind and onions into a smooth chutney.

3. Season with hot oil, put in mustard seeds, curry leaves, the roughly pounded garlic, and add the ground chutney. Add a little water while grinding.

4. Eat it with kadambutt or akki ooti.

# PARA

# Citron Para

### INGREDIENTS

*3 medium-sized citrons*

*1/2 cup sesame oil*

*10 cloves of garlic sliced*

*1 large piece ginger sliced*

*1/2 tsp mustard seeds*

*3 tbsp chilli powder*

*1/4 tsp fenugreek powder*

*1/4 tsp turmeric powder*

*salt to taste*

*1/2 cup vineger*

### METHOD

1. Put the citrons in boiling water with salt and turmeric powder.

2. After few minutes, strain the water, cut the citrons into cubes, rub salt on them and keep in the sun for 2 days.

3. Pour oil into a vessel, and when it is hot, fry the ginger and garlic. Next add mustard, chilli, fenugreek and turmeric powders and fry. Add citron and more salt, and lastly the vinegar. Mix well.

4. Store in airtight jars or bottles.

# Meen Para

1 kg fish cleaned, washed and cut into pieces

1 tbsp khus khus powdered

1 tbsp cumin powder

1/4 tsp fenugreek powder

1/4 tsp mustard powder

1/4 tsp pepper powder

4 cloves (powdered)

1 piece cinnamon (powdered)

15 kashmiri red chillies powdered, (roasted and kept aside)

**To keep aside:**

8 green chillies

8 cloves of garlic

1 large piece of ginger

1 cup oil

salt to taste

1/2 cup vinegar

1/2 tsp sugar

juice of 1 lemon

2 tsp chilli powder

## METHOD

1. Pour oil into a wok and deep fry the fish.
2. In another wok, heat the oil and add the masala. Add salt to taste and gently fry the masala. Add chilli powder, vinegar and sugar.

3. Take the pieces of fish and put into the fried masala. Take out and bottle. (The oil must float on the top.)

4. Instead of fish or meat brinjal and mushroom can also be used.

**For mutton, fish, brinjal, mushroom, pork**

*1 kg mutton*

*Mince green chillies and put in with mutton to cook.*

*Fry the meat like the fish and then add to the boiling gravy.*

*For brinjal or mushroom*

*Fry the brinjal or mushroom and put them into the boiling gravy.*

# Pandi Para

### INGREDIENTS

| |
|---|
| 1 kg pork with skin and fat cut into small pieces, washed and cleaned |
| 1/2 cup chilli powder |
| 1 tsp turmeric powder |
| 1 1/2 cups vinegar |
| 12 cloves of garlic each slit into two |
| 1 large piece ginger chopped |
| 1 tsp cumin powder |
| 1 tsp mustard powdered |
| salt to taste |
| 1 cup oil |
| 1 cup water |

### METHOD

1. Cook the pork pieces in 2 cups of water and one cup of vinegar. Dry them completely.
2. In 1 cup oil deep fry the pork pieces. Remove from fire.
3. In the same degchi, put in all the masala and fry over a low fire till the masala is cooked. Add the pork pieces and mix well. Cook till the gravy is thick, add more salt and vinegar. Bottle it when cold.

*Never overcook the pork. It should be medium done and should be actually cooked in the gravy.*

# GLOSSARY

| | | | | |
|---|---|---|---|---|
| koli | - chicken | | pachai mallu | - green chillies |
| yarchi | - mutton or any meat | | kooru | - rajma |
| kanne | - soup | | mangai | - mango |
| nalla mallu | - black pepper | | paji | - chutney |
| belai | - dal | | chakai | - raw jackfruit |
| puttus | - rice dishes | | kai pai kai | - bitter gourd |
| akki ooti | - rice chapati | | mudaray | - horse gram |
| nai kulu | - ghee rice | | koomu | - mushroom |
| mooru kulu | - curd rice | | muttai | - egg |
| pandi | - pork | | payasa | - kheer |
| chootad | - barbeque. | | baley | - banana |
| pooyarchi | - liver | | baley yale | - banana leaf (kolai) |
| kyma | - mince meat | | karjeekai | - sweet puffs |
| meen | - fish | | thindi | - snacks |
| tarakari | - vegetables | | para | - pickles |
| kay-boo | - yam leaves or patarvel | | | |

## Other Titles Published By Sterling

HPD 76E

*Vmc*